Anarchist Mexico

Anarchist Mexico

Ricardo Flores Magon & La Casa del Obrero

In the Mexican Revolution

Eric Leif Davin

DavinBooks
PO Box 90087
Pittsburgh, PA 15224

Anarchist Mexico
Ricardo Flores Magon & La Casa del Obrero
In the Mexican Revolution

ISBN 978-1-387-96014-9

Cover Photo by Tina Modotti

The Ideological Nature of the Revolution

Speaking of the 1910 Mexican Revolution, the first great revolution of the twentieth century, Frank Tannenbaum, once reputed to be "dean of the North American Mexicanists,"[1] declared that, "It would require great discernment to appraise even the more obvious events that have come from the armed rebellion initiated by Madero..."[2] Yet, just as Tannenbaum ignored his own caveat, so shall I in order to explore the same question he raised in his essay: The ideological nature of the Mexican Revolution. Specifically, I want to examine the contribution -- or lack thereof -- anarchism made to the Revolution. It is my contention that anarchism, as represented by the Mexican Liberal Party magonistas and the urban anarcho-syndicalist Casa del Obrero Mundial, had the potential to influence the ideological direction of the Revolution, but failed to do so through a combination of strategic errors on the parts of Liberal leader Ricardo Flores Magon and the leaders of the Casa del Obrero.

*****

According to Frank Tannenbaum, to speak of the ideological nature of the Revolution almost begs the question, for the Mexican Revolution, he asserted, was above all else, non-ideological. Unlike twentieth century revolutions which followed it, from the Russian to the Nazi to the Chinese to the Cuban to the Nicaraguan, the Mexican Revolution was unique in that it, "Had no philosophy, no political theory, and no official doctrine..."[3] Terming the Constitution of 1917 as, "The turning point," Tannenbaum said of it, "The program embodied in the Constitution is neither communist, socialist, fascist, syndicalist, nor liberal."[4]

Most commentators on the Revolution have either echoed Tannenbaum's assessment or read into the Revolution their own agenda.[5] Indeed, at times it has seemed that the Revolution was about, "a presidential interview, a candidate's book, because people were poor, because some were 'left out,' or because President Diaz had grown old and suffered from a toothache."[6] Thus, declared Arnaldo Cordova, we should think of the badly misnamed Mexican Revolution as merely a "populist" outburst. "In other words," he said, "it was *reformist* and not *revolutionary*."[7]

Mexican historian Moises Gonzalez Navarro is therefore almost an anomaly when, while describing the Revolution as basically a "jacquerie," he still found that ideology, in the form of urban anarchism, played a role in the Revolution and that, "With the organization of the Casa del Obrero Mundial (House of the Workers of the World), anarcho-syndicalism -- of Catalan origin -- achieved some importance which increased when the 'Red Battalions' participated in the armed conflict in support of Carranza."[8]

Nevertheless, the development of this anarcho-syndicalism, he claimed, owed virtually nothing to theoreticians and was a "spontaneous" and transient phenomenon. "The Mexican Revolution," agreed Villegas, "in reality, lacked great ideologists to shape it intellectually. The contribution of the so-called forerunners -- especially, Flores Magon and his associates -- was of far greater moral than ideological value...."[9]

Looking back from the present, this "non-ideological" revolution that began the twentieth century thus seems an aberration in the family of revolutions. How do we explain its curious development? Why was it those precursor theoreticians such as Flores Magon and the anarchism he advocated had so much less influence on the course of the Revolution than relative newcomers like Francisco Madero, with his minimal reformism?

Perhaps an answer can be found in the hostility of the United States government toward resident revolutionaries such as the magonistas and the relentlessly persecutory American legal system. At the outbreak of the Revolution, the future direction of the struggle was up for grabs:

> Revolutionary forces soon coalesced into two principal factions. The Liberals battled under the leadership of Ricardo Flores Magon, while the reformist Anti-Reelectionists, who had campaigned against Diaz's reelection in 1910, fought under wealthy landowner Francisco I. Madero. Flores Magon's supporters aimed to achieve a far more thorough overhaul of Mexico's political, social, and economic systems than did Madero's followers, who focused upon political changes....
>
> The Mexican Liberal Party, headquartered in Los Angeles, California, confronted ever increasing legal pressure from United States

> authorities at the prodding of Mexican officials.... United States authorities... became increasingly cooperative in the prosecution of the Liberals, for the United States government wished to foster favorable diplomatic relations with the moderate Madero to halt additional revolutionary destruction, and, at the same time, feared the spread of alien radicalism which already plagued the labor movement in the United States.[10]

Thus, the magonistas, who "...achieved highly visible military and propaganda successes, which revealed them as formidable contenders in the struggle to seize control of the Mexican government,"[11] were shunted aside over the course of the Revolution and became relegated to the periphery. To understand how this happened, let us look at a brief overview of their development.

The Rise and Fall of Ricardo Flores Magon

The young Ricardo Flores Magon, along with his older brother Jesus, first became active opponents to the Diaz dictatorship as students in May, 1892, when both were jailed for participating in anti-Diaz demonstrations in Mexico City. In August, 1900, the two brothers helped found the opposition newspaper *Regeneracion,* which later became the official voice of the Mexican Liberal Party and the virtual monopoly of Ricardo. The Liberal

Party itself, which was to become the most important opposition party, was founded on February 5, 1901 at a congress in San Luis Potosi organized by, among others, Antonio Diaz Soto y Gama. At this congress, Ricardo Flores Magon electrified the delegates by denouncing the Diaz dictatorship in a fiery speech that catapulted him to the forefront of the dissident movement.

From this point on, Magon was to face almost continuous official harassment and jailings, in both Mexico and the United States. Three months after his speech to the Liberal congress, Ricardo and his brother Jesus, along with their colleagues, were jailed for almost a year and "The Liberal leadership spent most of 1902 in prison as a result of continuing government efforts to silence the opposition."[12] This effort seems to have succeeded against Jesus, who dropped out of the opposition movement upon his release from prison, but he was replaced with Ricardo's younger brother Enrique, who was to share much of Ricardo's fate.

These two Magon brothers were again imprisoned from September, 1902 to January, 1903. By April, they were back in prison, to stay until October. Convinced that official repression and jailings would stifle further opposition in Mexico, the Liberal leadership, led by Soto y Gama, decided to continue the struggle from exile in the presumably more tolerant United States. In January, 1904, Ricardo Magon joined the Liberal leaders in Texas, never to return to Mexico during his life.

But the United States was soon revealed to be no more hospitable to revolutionary activities than was Mexico, as Magon would spend 13 of the next 19 years in

American prisons. When they were not in prison, the U.S. Postal Service, private detective agencies in the pay of Diaz, and a hostile American legal establishment pursued the Liberals from Texas to St. Louis (where the Magon brothers were briefly imprisoned) to Toronto to Montreal.

By 1906 the Magons were back in El Paso, where they organized an abortive revolt across the border. Fleeing El Paso authorities, who arrested other Liberal leaders for deportation to Mexico, Ricardo Magon turned up in Los Angeles, where he was jailed for a short time. Upon his release, he fled to San Francisco and thence to Sacramento to elude his pursuers.

In the meantime, great strikes erupted among copper miners at Cananea, Sonora, and among textile workers at Rio Blanco near Veracruz. Both are now viewed as portents of the coming Revolution, both were brutally repressed, and both involved organizers from Magon's Liberal Party. In 1906, at Cananea, 10,000 miners struck against the American-owned Green Consolidated Mining Company. Arizona Rangers were called in from across the border to restore order, but were not needed as the workers were massacred before the Americans arrived. Nevertheless, claims Leon Diaz Cardenas, Cananea marks the first appearance of "genuine class consciousness among the Mexican proletariat." Unquestionably, he says, quoting Teodoro Hernandez, "The Cananea strike was the primordial initiation of the social struggle in Mexico and it was due to the connection between the workers and the Organizing Junta of the Mexican Liberal Party."[13]

In the summer of 1907, Magon returned to Los Angeles, where Thomas Furlong, head of the Furlong Detective Agency, trapped him. Convicted of violating U.S. neutrality laws, Magon and other Liberal leaders spent the next three years in American prisons, first in Los Angeles, then in Yuma and Florence, Arizona. Thus, "The Mexican Liberal Party's leadership was crushed between 1907 and 1909," as they "spent the entire period working to untangle their legal problems."[14]

The three years Ricardo Magon spent in Arizona prisons were critical ones for Mexico. While Magon was removed from the scene, Mexico moved closer to revolution and reformist landowner Francisco Madero emerged as the leading opponent to the Diaz dictatorship. These were years Magon could not afford to lose, as he never truly regained his pre-eminent leadership position thereafter.

Magon then exacerbated his increasingly peripheral influence upon the evolving revolutionary movement by leading his fellow Liberals back to Los Angeles upon release from their Arizona imprisonment in 1910, "...even though the principal center of revolutionary activity was along the Texas border," where Madero was already operating from exile.[15] The American legal system was perhaps again responsible for this further marginalization of the magonistas, as warrants for their arrest for further violations of the neutrality laws were still outstanding in Texas.

When the Revolution began in earnest in the final months of 1910 and early 1911, magonista guerrilla bands were operating in the northern state of Chihuahua, but by mid-February, 1911, Madero had re-entered Mexico from

Texas with 130 men and absorbed the smaller magonista units into his own forces, "...thus ending the Mexican Liberal Party's opportunity for military victory on the mainland of Mexico."[16] Following this, Magon turned on Madero as a "traitor to the cause of liberty," a move that served only to further alienate Magon and his dwindling followers from the mainstream of the revolutionary struggle.

The final disaster for the Liberals, however, occurred in Baja California. In January 1911, the magonistas attempted to open a second front against Diaz in Baja California. Greatly augmented by American anarchists (including, legend has it, I.W.W. song writer Joe Hill), magonista forces seized Mexicali, Tijuana, and several lesser towns along the U.S.-Mexican border. After a lackluster six-month campaign, the Liberal army was driven out of Tijuana by federal troops in June. Most of the magonistas fled across the border, where they were arrested by patrolling U.S. Army units and imprisoned near San Diego.

Thus ended the magonista military effort, but the legal troubles of Ricardo Magon and the remaining Liberal leaders began anew. The dictator Diaz had now fled the country, but Madero, the "traitor to liberty," was in charge, and just as hostile to the Liberals as Diaz had been.

Upon their release from the Arizona State Penitentiary in 1910, the Mexican consul in Phoenix kept Magon and his comrades under close surveillance, even detailing their route back to Los Angeles. There the resident Mexican consul took up the task of surveillance and constant encouragement of swift American legal prosecution of the Liberals. Nothing changed after Madero's initial triumph of the Revolution. "After the decision to prosecute had been approved, an agent of the United States government was sent to obtain Madero's response to the action. Madero confidently replied that he welcomed the Liberals' prosecution..."[17] Thus, even before the fighting had ended in disaster for the Liberal army in Tijuana, Los Angeles police arrested Magon, his brother Enrique, and other Liberal leaders for violation of the neutrality laws in connection with the Baja California campaign.

After a year in detention, Magon and the Liberal leaders finally went on trial in June 1912. Their trial was characterized by the perjury of paid and coached prosecution witnesses, police harassment of defense witnesses, and prejudicial rulings by the presiding judge, which "Completely disrupted [the] defense."[18] On June 22, 1912, the all-Anglo jury returned a guilty verdict and the Magons and their comrades were sentenced to two years in prison. This was the Last Hurrah for the magonistas, as they were completely unable to re-establish themselves as part of the continuing Revolution when they returned from prison two years later.

Upon their release in 1914, the Magons returned to Los Angeles and established a commune on a five-acre farm for the handful of remaining Liberal activists. There they haphazardly published their newspaper, *Regeneracion,* for the next two years, only to be arrested once more in early 1916 for sending indecent articles ("material tending to incite murder, arson, or assassination") through the mail. The brothers were found guilty in June, 1916, and Ricardo was sentenced to a year in prison while Enrique, as the editor of the newspaper, was sentenced to three years.

In March, 1918, Ricardo was again arrested, this time for publishing an anarchist manifesto which purportedly violated the Espionage Act, the Trading-with-the-Enemy Act, and, again, the law against sending indecent material through the mails. Found guilty in July, the presiding judge declared that he viewed Magon "with particular and unusual disfavor" and that he deserved no pity because he refused to learn his lesson. Therefore, he sentenced Magon to 20 years in prison.

Magon was sent to Ft. Leavenworth penitentiary in Kansas where he died in his cell in ambiguous circumstances sometime in the early morning hours of November 21, 1922. In January, 1923, Ricardo Flores Magon at last ended his American exile as his body was shipped home to Mexico City.

High Noon in Baja

Absolutely crucial to the disruption of the magonistas and, therefore, to the ideological course of the Revolution, was the legal persecution of the magonistas by the United States government. Had it not imprisoned Ricardo and the other Liberal leaders for years at a time during the most formative period of the Revolution, it is likely that the magonistas -- and the anarchism Ricardo advocated -- may well have come to dominate the new Revolutionary government of Mexico with wide-ranging implications for the future.

But if constant harassment by the U.S. legal establishment was the crucial factor in the decline of magonista influence, why didn't Magon emulate so many other revolutionary leaders and escape it by crossing the border into Mexico at the head of his armed followers?

Ethel Duffy Turner, in her account of the magonista revolutionary struggle in Baja California, suggests that Magon was not *allowed* to return. "Certain sinister forces," she tells us, by which she means at this point Madero, "were well aware that Ricardo Flores Magon, if allowed to return to Mexico, could become a tremendous power on which to focus once again the revolutionary aims of the ordinary people. He could neither be bought off nor paid off with soft political jobs. Half blind, his health undermined by confinement in prisons but with his faculties of expression unimpaired, he was far too dangerous, in the eyes of certain elements to be allowed his well-deserved freedom."[19]

But what comes across far more graphically in her account is not that Magon wasn't *allowed* to return to Mexico from the United States, but that he consciously chose not to, as did, successfully, Madero, Pancho Villa in 1913 to oppose Huerta, and even Porfirio Diaz himself in 1876 to first establish his reign. Thus, the magonista military effort was rendered leaderless and prone to dissension and ultimately fatal lethargy.

Ethel Duffy Turner was not a professional historian, but an American supporter of Magon who first met him in Los Angeles in 1907 when she was 22 years old. Along with her husband, John Kenneth Turner, author of the influential exposè of the Diaz dictatorship, **Barbarous Mexico,** she worked on *Regeneracion,* the Liberal newspaper. However, both Turners broke with Magon on April 8, 1911, (an action never mentioned in

Turner's account of this period) because of Magon's increasing antagonism to Madero. That date happened to coincide with the publication in *Regeneracion* of a new Liberal Party manifesto, which for the first time clearly espoused Magon's anarchist beliefs, there-to-fore publicly sublimated. This increasing radicalism of Magon further alienated the Turners, who opposed the continued magonista military effort in Baja as well.

In her glorified account of the Baja campaign, however, Ethel Turner appears to be making amends for that unmentioned earlier rupture. In her highly partisan rendering, Ricardo Flores Magon is depicted as a romantic figure of saintly virtue, and there is little understanding of his political philosophy. Indeed, there is no discussion at all of Magon's political beliefs and one cannot glean from her work any idea of what the issues were which motivated Magon's struggle.

Instead, a picture as vague and non-ideological as the Mexican Revolution itself is purported to have been emerges, a picture of valiant and noble martyrs in revolt against evil incarnate. Turner's account of the Baja campaign is not the most detailed history of the Liberal military effort. For that, there is Lowell L. Blaisdell's **The Desert Revolution.**[20] However, Turner had the advantage of having known and worked with many of the participants personally, which lends an air of intimacy to her story.

The first Liberal military victories had been won by the charismatic young magonista Praxedis Guerrero, who crossed over into Mexico from Texas on December 19, 1910, with a handful of men to begin operating in Chihuahua. Revealingly, this action was taken on

Guerrero's own initiative and against the active opposition of Flores Magon, who wanted him to remain behind in Los Angeles -- as Magon was doing -- to continue working on the newspaper. This magonista military effort on the Mexican mainland suffered irreparable harm on December 30 when Guerrero was killed in battle and shortly thereafter Madero's forces in Chihuahua incorporated the magonista guerrillas into their own ranks.

Meanwhile, the Baja campaign had begun on January 28, 1911, when a miniscule Liberal "army" of either 14 or 17 men captured the border town of Mexicali. Within a short time, however, American Wobblies, as well as Canadian and even British anarchists and adventurers, who flocked across the border to aid in the revolutionary effort, swelled the Liberal ranks.

And it is at this point, with their first significant military success, that the magonista military failure began, for Magon did not cross over into Mexico and proclaim the newly captured town of Mexicali the headquarters of his movement. Instead, he remained in Los Angeles writing and editing his newspaper and attempted to direct the revolution long-distance through a revolving door of surrogate on-the-scene military leaders, which at one time even resulted in a deserting Federal army officer leading the rebel magonista forces. The result was lack of overall direction to the military effort and confusion as a series of contending *jefes* replaced each other at the head of the Liberal army.

Thus, for long periods of time the Liberal army did nothing, allowing the advantage of surprise and momentum to slip from its grasp. The Liberal army, for instance, never attacked Ensenada, the capitol of Baja and home of the major Federal military garrison, as Magon directed it to do from his headquarters in Los Angeles. Rather, led by a British adventurer, it took Tijuana instead, another border town, which was of no strategic significance, and allowed the Federal forces in Ensenada ample time to re-arm and reinforce themselves.

At the same time, the huge influx of Anglo volunteers greatly diluted the indigenous nature of the Liberal military effort. Indeed, not only was a large majority of the Liberal army officers Anglo, but even the Mexican rank and file combatants were essentially reduced to the status of a Mexican brigade in an Anglo army. And, without someone with the prestige of Magon himself on the scene to take these newcomers in hand, there was great confusion about the goals of the revolt. This new recruits, "Either did not read the paper [*Regeneracion*] or did not digest its contents,"[21] and so knew virtually nothing about why they were supposed to be fighting. "In the minds of many was confusion as to the ultimate aims of the Partido Liberal."[22]

By the time Federal troops routed the Liberal army from Tijuana on June 22, 1911, the magonista military effort had already ground to a halt. Lacking both political and military coherence and direction from the absent Magon, it was never able to take advantage of its initial victories. Magon was revealed to be an abysmal failure as a military leader -- and therein lay the failure of anarchistic magonismo to attain any significant military and, thus, ideological influence over the course of the Revolution.

To a certain extent, Ward Sloan Albro, III agrees with this assessment. "Flores Magon did not and could not succeed as a revolutionary leader in Mexico," he claims. "He was a writer, not a leader in the field."[23] He contends that, "As his aspirations became more sublime, his followers became fewer. By the end of the year, he had become virtually a leader without a following.... Mexico listened to Flores Magon of 1906, not the Flores Magon of 1910."[24]

And yet, in the end, Albro's reasoning seems insufficient to explain why Magon's anarchism did not become more influential. Albro is clearly philosophically opposed to anarchism, as when he states categorically that, "Flores Magon was doomed to failure in 1910. Possibly his [anarchistic] goals will always be doomed to failure."[25] Anarchism, in other words, is merely an unattainable utopian dream.[26]

But Albro never really makes clear exactly *why* Magon was "doomed to failure." In opposition to the viability of an anarchist Mexican Revolution, Albro hypothesizes that, "Had he [Magon] moved into Mexico leading a revolutionary force and demanding an economic revolution, Madero and the men who made the Madero revolution a success may well have rallied to the support of the dictatorship.... Had they failed to stop such a revolt in 1910, the United States...most certainly would have intervened."[27]

Perhaps this projected scenario may indeed have come about. However, it does not explain *why* the Revolution failed to develop in this ideological direction, it only guesses at what might have been the American *reaction* to such a direction. Instead, it makes sense to conclude that the reason anarchism did not take root in the deserts of northern Mexico during the opening stages of the Revolution was due to the failure of the anarchist leader, Magon, to cross into Mexico and exploit his initial military victories. He was a leader who refused to lead his army.

But Flores Magon was not the only exponent of anarchism in the Revolution and the triumph of this ideology did not depend upon him alone. While his army was fighting and losing in the deserts of Baja, another urban-based working class anarchism was taking shape in the heart of Mexico. This anarchism was that of the Casa del Obrero Mundial -- The House of the Workers of the World -- based in Mexico City. Even with the failure of magonismo in northern Mexico, the Casa del Obrero held out the significant possibility of imparting an ideological orientation to the Revolution. Why, then, did this not happen? For the answer, we must look to the contingent shifting political alliances of the revolutionary struggle itself.

The Casa del Obrero and the Red Battalions

John Mason Hart has disagreed with the reputed non-ideological nature of the Revolution. Instead -- claiming that American investors owned 22% of Mexican land in 1910 -- Hart describes the Revolution as, "The first Third World uprising against American economic penetration and control," and argues that ideologically class conscious activity on the part of insurgent groups, largely overlooked by most historians of the Revolution, played a large role in the struggle.[28] That this activity has not been adequately acknowledged Hart attributes to the fact that the eventual victors in the Revolution were the provincial elites represented by the Constitutionalist Sonoran Dynasty. These "new bosses" submerged revolutionary ideologies under the mythology of *no* ideology in order to domesticate the Revolution.[29]

Nevertheless, the Revolution had several ideologically radical constituencies. Hart examined four separate Mexican socio-economic groups -- the peasantry, urban industrial workers, provincial elites, and the "pequena burguesia" (petty bourgeoisie) -- and finds that they all had ample economic reasons to revolt. It was among the peasants and the urban workers, however, that class-conscious ideologies, and especially anarchism, took root.

Fifty miles outside of Mexico City in the state of Morelos, for instance, where Emiliano Zapata operated for so long, "The Morelos peasantry were affected not only by the efforts of metropolitan and foreign capitalists but also by the diffusion of European radical ideas. Nationalism, anarchism, and liberalism found a receptive audience there. Zapata acknowledged his debt to them in his myriad proclamations, "al pueblo Mexicano," while incorporating anarchist advisors from the revolutionary workers' organization, the Casa del Obrero Mundial."[30]

Similarly, among the industrial working class, "Worker unrest rooted in colonial-era immiseration and artisan leadership found anarcho-syndicalism a solution."[31] The foremost organizational expression of this anarcho-syndicalism was to be found in the Casa del Obrero Mundial, organized by, among others, Liberal Party activist, Flores Magon compatriot, and Zapata advisor Antonio Diaz Soto y Gama. During the fall of 1914, the Casa launched "an intense organizing" campaign among urban workers and "grew with extreme rapidity."[32] By February, 1915, the Casa represented 50,000 urban workers.

Thus, dissident class-based ideology in fact motivated much of the lower-class agitation, both in the cities and out in the countryside, before and during the Revolution. That this ideologically-informed unrest did not have a more influential role in determining the course of the Revolution Hart attributes to the fact that there were no viable organizational links between the two movements, thus making them -- and the Revolution -- vulnerable to American intervention. "Formally constituted political parties," he says, "possessed little of the organizational strength and unity between peasants and industrial workers that characterized later struggles in Russia and China."[33] Thus, although individuals such as Diaz Soto y Gama -- a founder of Casa Obrero and advisor to Zapata -- favored an alliance of the urban and rural working classes, no organizational link was constructed between the two.

Therefore, despite the seeming mutuality of interests between the urban Casa and the villista-zapatista peasant armies, the Casa threw its strength behind the Constitutionalist forces, the heirs of Modero's reformism, which were making sympathetic noises. The decisive blow to ideological radicalism among the compartmentalized urban workers and the rural agrarians came when "The alarmed American government decisively affected the outcome of the revolution through a secret and massive infusion of arms during its 1914 intervention at Veracruz."[34] All of these munitions and arms were channeled to the Constitutionalist forces representing the provincial elites: "Equipped with modern artillery, machine guns, barbed wire, trucks, radio transmitters, and rifles, they quickly succeeded in defeating the much larger but less well-equipped Villista and Zapatista main forces directed by mostly rural working-class leaders."[35]

Following the strategic defeat of the rural-based radicals, the provincial elites then turned upon the urban radicals, beginning in mid-1915. The Casa del Obrero Mundial had, "...planned eventually to seize control of Mexico's private enterprises and to reorganize them on an anarcho-syndicalist basis.... Increasingly militant and large-scale strikes, mass demonstrations and street violence continued for fifteen months.... The unrest finally ended in August 1916 when troops broke the second general strike of that year, smashed the various Casa centers located in the nation's cities, and with them the power of the revolutionary urban labor movement."[36]

However, at the time of the initial alliance with the Constitutionalists, it had seemed that Constitutionalist leader Venustiano Carranza offered genuine hope to the urban syndicalists. By the fall of 1914, Carranza had essentially been reduced to his stronghold in Veracruz on the Gulf of Mexico, although a few other areas were still loyal to him. It was at this time that he made a bold move to gain the allegiance of the Casa.

The organized urban workers comprised a vast untapped manpower reserve that had thus far refused to join the revolutionary struggle on any side because it saw "politics" as a betrayal of its anarcho-syndicalist principles. In order to enlist this reserve in his struggle, Carranza issued his Decree of December 12, 1914, which essentially called for "the equality of all Mexicans," especially the urban workers. In this sense, claims Jose Mancisidor, the Decree was "a profound reformation of the ideas behind the Plan of Guadalupe." It was a radical move that, says Mancisidor, "created a new historical condition in the country" and succeeded in attracting the Casa to Carranza's side, forcing it to abandon its principled neutrality toward the "political" struggle.[37]

Additionally, however, "The Casa leadership... reasoned that the Constitutionalist movement...was a likely winner," and felt that an alliance with it would give the Casa carte blanche to organize urban workers after the war.[38] Phrased thus, the association seems a bit opportunist, but Rosendo Salazar, a pro-alliance Casa leader at the time, argued that it was a necessary step. To this point, he approvingly quoted Gonzalo Mazon de Pedro who claimed, "Madero had been a victim of treason, but the Casa del Obrero Mundial, continuing the social struggle, survived and the pact of incorporation with the Constitutionalist Army was judged to be an obligation."[39]

Jesus Silva Herzog further argued that Casa was obliged to "abandon its merely syndicalist struggle" and side with Carranza because the Constitutionalist package "seemed to offer major guarantees for the attainment of their ideals for social transformation. For this reason, at that precise historical moment and geographic location, Carranza represented the Revolution and Villa the contrary."[40]

Still, as Jose Luis Reyna and Marcelo Miquet Fleury remind us, there were some in Casa who objected to the alliance. "Without doubt," they say, "the pact was not unanimously accepted by la Casa: An opposing faction argued against the loss of their autonomy and, therefore, the loss of their maneuverability in relation to the State. Nevertheless, they were not able to stop the creation of the Red Battalions."[41]

Subsequently, six "Red Battalions" of Casa combatants, totaling 15,000 men, were organized to fight in the Constitutionalist army, thus providing the personnel at a crucial juncture to operate the American weaponry stockpiled at Veracruz. These American munitions "turned the tide of the revolution," and, as "the main forces of the urban and rural sectors, divided by ancestry, culture, and class interests, turned on each other" in 1914 and 1915, "American intervention eliminated any possibility of victory for the rural working class."[42]

However, the *urban* working class still retained a possibility of both political and military victory. Organized into numerous labor syndicates, with armed militias at their disposal, and with "The most radical leadership imaginable in Latin America at that time," the anarcho-syndicalist Casa posed a serious threat to the newly victorious Constitutionalist government.[43]

Reyna and Fleury seem to agree with this assessment of growing Casa strength. "The participation of la Casa in the Constitutionalist triumph," they write, "was reflected in a great numerical and geographic expansion of la Casa. In any one territory they conquered for the Constitutionalists, they established a branch of la

Casa.... And they declared that they still adhered to their ancient anarchist principles, proclaimed the organization of a workers' congress with the aim of creating a General Confederation of Workers affiliated with the International, diffused rationalist doctrines among the workers in schools and established strong syndicates to defend the rights of the workers."[44]

Indeed, Jorge Basurto seems to agree with this assessment. Following the February, 1915 formal alliance between the Constitutionalist forces and the Casa, he says, the latter made rapid progress in organizing urban workers. "Very quickly," he writes, there appeared Casa subsidiaries, "all with the same basic structure," in towns throughout Mexico: "The idea of syndicalism proclaimed by COM [Casa del Obrero Mundial] prospered rapidly throughout the Republic and resulted in the establishment of a multitude of syndicates: Street-car drivers, bricklayers, teamsters, mechanics, blacksmiths, etc.; there was almost no occupation which did not have its syndicate."[45] In addition, claims Basurto, there were strikes among electrical workers in Guadalajara and gold miners in Mexico State, and many lockouts in Veracruz, Puebla, and the Federal District, all ostensibly provoked by the Casa.

Thus, strikes, demonstrations, and street violence escalated throughout 1915 as, "The anarcho-syndicalist Casa leaders demanded workers' control of production, wages, and prices.... No era in the history of Mexican labor has witnessed the working-class solidarity and belligerence that the Casa members, now over 100,000 in number and moving toward 150,000, demonstrated in 1915 and 1916."[46]

To forestall a developing working class revolution of an anarcho-syndicalist nature, the Constitutionalist government disbanded the Red Battalions in January, 1916, and arrested Casa leaders throughout the nation. The Casa responded with a general strike in May, 1916 and another in the summer of 1916. Initially successful, the summer strike was crushed and, with it, so were the last hopes of a successful "red" revolution in Mexico.

Revolutionary Possibilities

What finally emerged from the Mexican Revolution was a victory of the provincial elites who rejected the anarchism of both Ricardo Flores Magon and the Casa del Obrero. If these elites had any ideology, it was merely the tepid ideology of transferring Mexico's wealth from American hands to their own. It was this "nationalistic" ideology which then relegated anarchism to "utopian" irrelevancy and proclaimed that all the Revolution had really sought was its own triumph -- the triumph of what Villegas said was, "Nothing but a democratic, popular, nationalist movement."

But, it seems clear there did exist the potential for a more ideologically radical outcome of the Revolution. On the eve of the Revolution, Ricardo Flores Magon and his followers seemed poised to play a significant role. During the Revolution itself, the Casa del Obrero and the Red Battalions for a brief moment held the balance of power. Had Flores Magon followed the lead of other revolutionaries, such as Pancho Villa or even Francisco Madero, and abandoned the United States for the battlefield as soon as his forces captured Mexicali, it seems likely the magonista army would not have dissolved into confusion and he, himself, would not have died in an American prison. But, agrees Manuel Gonzalez Ramirez, "Flores Magon, never boldly crossed the frontier in order to enter the national territory and captain the revolt, thus arousing his partisans. Instead, he provoked violence by remote control. This decision carried defeat and, finally, a life of solitude."[47]

Similarly, had la Casa del Obrero followed the urging of leaders such as former magonista Antonio Diaz Soto y Gama and forged an alliance with rural revolutionaries Villa and Zapata, instead of Sonoran elitists Carranza and Obregon, it is possible Soto y Gama himself may have one day become President and urban anarcho-syndicalism a major ideological defining element of the Mexican Revolution.

Had either of these contingencies developed, then instead of the Mexican Revolution being known today by many, if not most, historians as a "reformist," "non-ideological" revolution, it might instead have been the twentieth century's first great ideological explosion.

---

[1]Ross, Stanley R., Ed., **Is The Mexican Revolution Dead?,** Temple University Press: Philadelphia, 1975, 1966, p. 195.

[2]Tannenbaum, Frank, "Some Reflections on the Mexican Revolution," in Ross, p. 196. Originally in *Journal of International Affairs,* IX, 1, 1955.

[3]Tannenbaum, p. 200.

[4]Tannenbaum, p. 201.

[5]For instance, Stanley Ross agreed with Tannenbaum when he stated that, "A key element in the explanation of the character of this upheaval is to be found in the absence, in large measure, of a prior or even accompanying ideology." See Ross, p. 9.

According to Howard F. Cline, "It is necessary to stress that the Mexican Revolution boasts no Marx or Engels to provide an ideology in advance and that its doctrines change from time to time..." See Howard F. Cline, "Mexico: A Matured Latin American Revolution, 1910-1960," in Ross, p. 66. Originally in *The Annals of the American Academy of Political and Social Science,* CCCXXXIII, January, 1961.

Jose Iturriaga also concurred that, "the Mexican Revolution lacked a single plan." See Jose Iturriaga, "Mexico and Its Historic Crisis," in Ross, p. 89. Originally in *Cuadernos Americanos,* XXXIII, May-June, 1947.

So, too, did Daniel Cosio Villegas claim that, "The Mexican Revolution never had a clear program...[being] nothing but a democratic, popular, nationalist movement..." See Daniel Cosio Villegas, "Mexico's Crisis," in Ross, pp. 74, and 75. Originally in *Cuadernos Americanos,* XXXII, March-April, 1947.

If it was anything at all, stressed Jose Mancisidor, it was "a popular bourgeois revolution, antifeudal and anti-imperialist..." See Jose Mancisidor, **Historia de la Revolucion Mexicana,** Costa-Amic Editores: Mexico, D.F., 1957, 1981, p. 313.

Nebulous generalities come even from those who might have been expected to offer a more ideological description of the Revolution. Radical labor leader Vicente Lombardo Toledano, for example, seemed to agree with Mancisidor in describing the Revolution as merely, "...a popular movement tending toward the destruction of feudalism." See Vicente Lombardo Toledano, "A Democracy of the People," in Ross, p. 167. Originally in *Problemas Agricolas e Industriales de Mexico,* VIII, 2, April-June 1955.

Meanwhile, Antonio Diaz Soto y Gama, renowned as an early member of the magonista Liberal Party, a founder of Mexico City's syndicalist workers' organization Casa del Obrero Mundial, and a zapatista ideologue, declared that, "The Revolution was not undertaken for any one class, party, oligarchy, or group. The Revolution was undertaken to achieve freedom and well being for all Mexicans -- to obtain the physical, intellectual, and moral progress of all the inhabitants of Mexico, regardless of race, creed, ideology, class, or political or social rank.... The Revolution was and continues to be an upward impulse, a continuous force, a current of life..." See Antonio Diaz Soto y Gama, "A thorough Attack on the Revolution," in Ross, pp. 135, and 136. Originally in *El Universal,* Nov. 17, 1943.

And what was the goal of this "non-ideological" revolution? President Alvaro Obregon claimed the Revolution was fought merely to give the average Mexican more of a say in government. See Alvaro Obregon, "The Revolution Was Fought for Democracy," in Charles C. Cumberland, Ed., **The Meaning of the Mexican Revolution,** D.C. Heath & Co.: Boston, 1967, pp. 9-14. Originally in Alvaro Obregon, **La Caida de Carranza: de la dictadura a la libertad,** Mexico City, 1920, pp. 3-26.

According to Guanajuato labor leader Nicolas Cano, the Revolution was fought to win the right to strike. See Nicolas Cano, "The Revolution Was Fought to Equalize Capital and Labor," in Cumberland, pp. 4-9. Originally in Nicolas Cano, **Diario de los debates del congreso Constituyente,** Mexico City, 1922, pp. 607-610, 616.

For Luis Cabrera, President Venustiano Carranza's Finance Minister, the struggle was fought vaguely for "liberty, development and welfare." See Luis Cabrera, "The Revolution is Constructive," in Cumberland, p. 1. Originally in *The Annals of the American Academy of Political and Social Science,* January, 1917, pp. 11-17.

Meanwhile, Iturriaga said its main goals were, "The replacement of an immoderate working day by one of eight hours...the construction of schools...effective suffrage...[and] destruction of the feudal agrarian society." See Iturriaga, in Ross, p. 89.

[6]Hart, John Mason, **Revolutionary Mexico: The Coming and Process of the Mexican Revolution,** University of California Press: Berkeley, 1987, p. ix.

[7]Cordova, Arnaldo, **La ideologia de la Revolucion Mexicana: La formacion del nuevo regimen,** Ediciones Era: Mexico, D.F., 1973, p. 37.

[8]Navarro, Moises Gonzalez, "The Ideology of the Mexican Revolution," in Ross, p. 182. Originally in *Historia Mexicana,* XI, 4, April-June 1961.

[9]Cosio Villegas, Daniel, "The Mexican Revolution, Then And Now," in Ross, p. 118. Originally in **Change in Latin America: The Mexican and Cuban Revolutions,** 1960 Montgomery Lectureship on Contemporary Civilization, University of Nebraska Press: Lincoln, 1961, pp. 23-37.

[10]Langham, Thomas C., **Border Trials: Ricardo Flores Magon and The Mexican Liberals,** Texas Western Press, The University of Texas: El Paso, 1981, p. 6.

[11]Langham, p. 6.

[12]Langham, p. 11.

[13]Hernandez, Teodoro, *La Patria,* Mexico, D.F., 16 de noviembre 1931, quoted in Leon Diaz Cardenas, **Cananea: Primer brote de sindicalismo en Mexico,** Secretaria del Trabajo y Prevision Social: Mexico, D.F., 1986, 1936, pp. 7, 85.

[14]Langham, p. 25.

[15]Langham, p. 27.

[16]Langham, pp. 29-30.

[17]Langham, p. 39.

[18]Langham, p. 47.

[19]Turner, Ethel Duffy, **Revolution in Baja California: Ricardo Flores Magon's High Noon,** Edited and Annotated by Rey Devis, Blaine Ethridge Books: Detroit, no publication date, but probably after 1976, p. 83.

[20]Blaisdell, Lowell L., **The Desert Revolution: Baja California, 1911,** University of Wisconsin Press: Madison, 1962.

[21]Turner, p. 37.

[22]Turner, p. 37.

[23]Albro, III, Ward Sloan, **Ricardo Flores Magon and the Liberal Party: An Inquiry into the Origins of the Mexican Revolution of 1910,** unpublished doctoral dissertation, University of Arizona: Tucson, 1967, p. x.

[24]Albro, p. 193, 191.

[25]Albro, p. 227.

[26]In this opinion, it seems Albro has plenty of company. Arnaldo Cordova, for instance, dismissed Magon as simply, "A utopian revolutionary." See Cordova, p. 173.

Likewise, Manuel Gonzalez Ramirez believes "The magonista tragedy" was Magon's adherence to "the utopia of anarchism" and "the socialist utopia," which had no concurrence with the direction in which Mexico was headed. See Manuel Gonzalez Ramirez, **La Revolucion Social de Mexico: Las ideas - La violencia,** Fondo de Cultura Economica: Mexico, D.F., 1960, pp. 83, 107, 439.

In retrospect, however, the contingent nature of history is usually forgotten and lost causes are always deemed "utopian." Whatever happens is seen as inevitable after the fact.

[27]Albro, p. 226.
[28]Hart, p. 18.
[29]Hart, p. 17.
[30]Hart, p. 7.
[31]Hart, p. 9.
[32]Hart, p. 303.
[33]Hart, p. 12.
[34]Hart, p. x.
[35]Hart, p. 15.
[36]Hart, p. 15.
[37]Mancisidor, p. 280-281.
[38]Hart, p. 307.
[39]Mazon de Pedro, Gonzalo, "El Anarquismo," *Pensamiento Politico,* num. 5, Vol. II, septiembre 1969, quoted in Rosendo Salazar, **Antecedentes del movimiento obrero revolucionario en Mexico: Los anos convulsos,** Biblioteca del Instituto Nacional de Estudios Historicos de la Revolucion Mexicana: Mexico, D.F., 1973, p. 89.
[40]Herzog, Jesus Silva, **Breve historia de la Revolucion Mexicana: La etapa Constitucionalista y la lucha de facciones,** Fondo de Cultura Economica: Mexico, D.F., 1960, p. 143.
[41]Reyna, Jose Luis, y Marcelo Miquet Fleury, "Introduccion a la historia de las organizaciones obreras en Mexico: 1912-1966," en **Tres estudios sobre el movimiento obrero en Mexico,** El Colegio de Mexico: Mexico, D.F., 1976, p. 16.
[42]Hart, p. 312.
[43]Hart, p. 314.
[44]Reyna y Fleury, p. 18. The authors state that the Red Battalions established branches of la Casa in Yucatan, Campeche, Tabasco, Chiapas, Tehuantepec, Veracruz, Tamaulipas, Queretaro, Jalisco, Hidalgo, Colima, Nuevo Leon, and Michoacán, among other places.
[45]Basurto, Jorge, **El proletariado industrial en Mexico (1850-1930),** Universidad Nacional Autonoma de Mexico: Mexico, D.F., 1975, p.

173. The list of places in which Basurto says Casa subsidiaries were established include Orizaba, Pachuca, Morelia, Monterrey, Queretaro, San Luis Potosi, Merida, Cordoba, Jalapa, San Andres Tuxtla, Tlacotalpan, Puerto Mexico, Oaxaca, Tapachula, Tehuantepec, Irapuato, Leon, Colima, Tampico, Arbol Grande, Dona Cecilia, Ciudad Victoria, Nuevo Laredo, Saltillo, Torreon, Sonora and Chihuahua.

[46]Hart, p. 314, 315.

[47]Ramirez, p. 441.

www.ingramcontent.com/pod-product-compliance
Ingram Content Group UK Ltd.
Pitfield, Milton Keynes, MK11 3LW, UK
UKHW040028200726
13854UKWH00001B/411

9 781387 960149